The Remote Sales Leader: Building High-Performing Teams

Derek Simon

Table of Contents

Chapter 1: Introduction to Sales Call Center Leadership

What is the Role of a Team Lead?

A remote call center leader plays a crucial role in managing and overseeing the operations of a virtual call center team. They are responsible for ensuring that the team delivers exceptional customer service, meets sales performance targets, and maintains a high level of employee engagement.

The primary responsibility of a remote call center leader is to establish a strong communication system within the team. This involves setting up regular check-ins, video conferences, and other communication channels to ensure that all team members are well-informed about their tasks, goals, and any changes in company policies or procedures. Effective communication is paramount in a remote environment, as it helps to bridge the physical gap between team members and fosters a sense of unity and collaboration.

A remote call center leader must continuously monitor key performance indicators (KPIs) to evaluate the team's progress and identify areas for improvement. This includes tracking metrics such as call handling time, customer satisfaction scores, and first-call resolution rates. By analyzing these metrics, the leader can develop strategies to enhance the team's overall performance, provide constructive feedback, and offer targeted coaching to individual team members.

A remote call center leader must create a positive work environment that encourages team members to stay motivated and engaged. This can be achieved through regular recognition of individual achievements, offering opportunities for professional development, and promoting a healthy work-life balance. Additionally, the leader should foster a culture of open feedback and support, enabling team members to voice their concerns and suggestions for improvement.

They are responsible for implementing and maintaining customer service standards that align with the company's values and objectives. This involves training team members on best practices, monitoring calls for quality assurance, and addressing any customer complaints or escalations promptly. The leader must also stay up to date with industry trends and customer expectations to ensure the team's service delivery remains competitive and relevant.

A remote call center leader must be prepared to adapt to changes in technology, customer preferences, and industry standards. They should be proactive in identifying opportunities for process improvements, implementing new tools and technologies, and streamlining workflows to enhance efficiency. By embracing change and fostering a culture of continuous improvement, the remote call center leader can ensure the long-term success of the team and the satisfaction of its customers.

Importance of Leadership in a Sales Call Center

Effective Leadership Sets the Tone:
In a remote sales call center, effective leadership is crucial for setting the tone and fostering a positive work environment. Strong leaders establish clear expectations, communicate efficiently, and provide the necessary support for their team members to excel. By modeling professionalism and enthusiasm, leaders can inspire their remote sales agents to perform at their best, ultimately driving higher sales and customer satisfaction.

Navigating Challenges in Remote Settings:
Remote sales call centers present unique challenges, such as the lack of face-to-face interactions and potential feelings of isolation among team members. Effective leaders recognize and address these challenges by implementing strategies to maintain team cohesion, such as regular video conferences, team-building activities, and creating opportunities for informal communication. By fostering a sense of camaraderie and collaboration, leaders can help their team adapt to the remote work environment and stay motivated.

Empowering Agents through Training and Development:
Strong leadership in a remote sales call center involves empowering agents with the knowledge and tools required to succeed. By providing comprehensive training, ongoing development opportunities, and constructive feedback, leaders equip their team with the skills and confidence needed to excel in their roles. This investment in employee growth not only enhances the team's overall performance but also increases job satisfaction and employee retention.

Data-Driven Decision Making:
In a remote sales call center, effective leaders rely on data-driven decision-making

to optimize performance and drive results. By tracking and analyzing key performance indicators (KPIs), leaders can identify areas for improvement, allocate resources efficiently, and set realistic goals for their team. By sharing these insights with their team, leaders can foster a culture of continuous improvement and create a shared understanding of the organization's objectives.

Adaptable and Resilient Leadership

The dynamic nature of remote sales call centers requires leaders to be adaptable and resilient. As technology, customer needs, and market conditions evolve, leaders must be prepared to adjust their strategies and tactics accordingly. By staying informed about industry trends and best practices, leaders can ensure their team remains competitive and agile in the face of change. This adaptability not only benefits the remote sales call center's performance but also demonstrates to team members the importance of embracing change and staying ahead of the curve.

Key Qualities of an Effective Leader

Strong Communication Skills

An effective leader in a remote sales call center must possess exceptional communication skills. This includes not only the ability to convey information clearly and concisely, but also to actively listen and understand the needs and concerns of their team members. With remote work, communication can be more challenging, making it essential for leaders to utilize various channels such as email, video calls, and instant messaging to maintain open lines of communication and ensure that everyone is on the same page.

Adaptability and Flexibility

In a remote sales call center, leaders must be adaptable and flexible in order to respond to the ever-changing needs of their team and business environment. This includes being open to new technologies, adjusting to different time zones, and adapting to the unique challenges that remote work presents. By demonstrating a willingness to embrace change and learn from it, leaders can foster a resilient and innovative team culture that thrives in the face of adversity.

Empathy and Emotional Intelligence

An effective remote sales call center leader must demonstrate empathy and emotional intelligence. This involves understanding the emotions and motivations of their team members, as well as being able to manage their own emotions effectively. By showing empathy and providing support, leaders can create a positive and inclusive work environment that encourages team members to perform at their best. Emotional intelligence also helps leaders to recognize and address potential conflicts or issues before they escalate, ensuring that the team remains focused and productive.

Goal Setting and Performance Management

Effective leaders in a remote sales call center must be adept at setting clear, achievable goals and managing the performance of their team members. This involves regularly monitoring progress, providing constructive feedback, and celebrating accomplishments. By establishing a strong performance management system, leaders can ensure that their team remains motivated and engaged, while also identifying areas for improvement and growth. Additionally, setting realistic expectations and providing the necessary resources for success helps to foster a culture of accountability and high performance.

Building and Maintaining Trust

Trust is a crucial component of successful remote sales call center leadership. Leaders must work to establish and maintain trust with their team members by being transparent, consistent, and reliable. This includes sharing information openly, following through on commitments, and treating team members with respect and fairness. By fostering a trusting relationship with their team, leaders can create a positive and collaborative work environment where team members feel comfortable sharing ideas, taking risks, and working together to achieve common goals.

As a sales call center leader, effectively guiding your team is critical to success. By demonstrating key leadership qualities like vision, integrity and motivation, a call center leader can inspire high performance and empower agents to exceed goals. operative leadership helps create a productive culture where new sales are delivered, and customer experiences shine. Although the role of a leader is challenging, building a winning team and achieving meaningful results make the efforts worthwhile. The future of a sales call center depends on strong leadership today.

Chapter 2: Building a High-Performing Sales Team

Building a Team

The sound of ringing phones echoed through the walls of the remote sales call center, signaling another day of potential sales opportunities. But as the world began to shift toward remote work, the traditional methods of building and managing a high-performing sales team were no longer viable.

Gone were the days of face-to-face meetings, team huddles, and daily check-ins. Now, managers had to figure out how to create and maintain high morale, productivity, and a sense of belonging in their teams from hundreds of miles away.

This book aims to guide managers on how to build a successful sales team that can thrive in a remote work environment. We'll delve into strategies for hiring the right people for the job, developing an effective onboarding process, implementing communication tools and techniques that foster collaboration and engagement, tracking performance metrics, providing consistent feedback, and ultimately achieving their goals.

So if you find yourself struggling with managing a remote sales team or looking to improve its effectiveness, buckle up and let's dive in.

Recruiting and Hiring Top Talent

A Team Lead in a remote call center plays a crucial role in recruiting and hiring top talent. Their role involves identifying the needs of the call center and finding suitable candidates who can fulfill these needs efficiently. They often act as the first point of contact for job applicants, answering initial queries and explaining what is required from the role.

Team Leads are also responsible for screening resumes, conducting phone screenings, arranging interviews with the HR department, and conducting initial assessments to determine if an applicant meets the call center's requirements. This process requires excellent communication skills, problem-solving abilities, and strong attention to detail.

Team Leads also play a vital role in maintaining a positive candidate experience throughout the recruitment process. They ensure that candidates receive prompt feedback and updates on their application status. Additionally, they follow up with unsuccessful candidates in a professional and respectful manner.

Once new hires have been selected, Team Leads help onboard them into the organization. This includes providing new hires with relevant information about the company's culture, policies, procedures, and systems. Team Leads may also work closely with the HR department to ensure that training programs are in place to develop team members' skills.

In summary, a Team Lead is a critical player in recruiting and hiring top talent in a remote call center. They identify staffing needs and work hard to identify candidates who possess the right combination of skills and qualities to excel in this environment. They also ensure a positive candidate experience throughout the recruitment process, while supporting new hires through their onboarding journey.

Developing Team Culture & Values

A call center team lead plays a critical role in developing team culture and values in a remote call center. In this modern workplace, where remote working has become the norm, it's more important than ever for Team Leads to foster team culture that will benefit the entire organization.

Team Leads set the tone for their team members by exemplifying company values, following company policies and creating a positive environment. They act as an intermediary between upper management and their peers by emphasizing the importance of following policies without undermining individuality.

The Team Lead creates trust and open communication between team members by ensuring active participation of all employees through virtual meetings, document sharing platforms and team chats. This helps build healthy team relationships that encourage collaboration and a sense of community within the team.

They also provide support and guidance to team members to ensure they have the necessary tools to succeed at their work while maintaining a good work-life balance in remote working environments. This helps maintain morale, improves employee retention rates and the overall efficiency of the operation.

In addition, a Team Leader builds an interactive feedback system among teammates and implements motivational activities like incentives, gamification etc. This collective approach ensures tasks go beyond just monitoring employee performance to building a connection between people working remotely from one another even if separated by various time zones.

Lastly, Grooming efficiencies by adopting smart technologies; analyzing areas where changes would boost productivity, streamlining operations could decrease potential tensions. Resolving issues quickly and coaching staff on areas causing conflicts fall under the responsibilities of the Team Lead in remote call centers.

Everything that is outlined above creates a blueprint of the integral role played by Team Leads in developing team culture and values in a remote call center. Their ability to be empathetic, efficient communicators and self-motivated leaders is vital for keeping workers feeling connected and heard- leading to increased productivity, better satisfaction levels amongst workers and improved business outcomes over time.

Setting Goals and Expectations

A sales team lead in a remote call center plays a pivotal role in setting goals and expectations for their team. Here are five important ways in which they do so:

1. **Defining Sales Targets:** The Sales Team Lead is responsible for defining targets for the team, based on the organization's objectives. They establish key performance indicators and revenue goals in line with the company's business plan, which guide agents' work as they make outbound calls or handle inbound leads.

2. **Communicating Expectations:** A remote work environment can create communication barriers, but a good Sales Team Lead overcomes these by providing clear expectations to their team. They ensure that the agents understand what's required of them, including metrics like average handling time (AHT), registration conversion, and transfer rate.

3. Monitoring Performance: In a remote call center, the Sales Team Lead must monitor each agent's performance closely. They use tools like call recordings, dashboards, and scorecards to review sales and productivity metrics. Based on this data, they provide feedback to help agents improve their work, address any issues promptly and ensure everyone is meeting their goals.

4. Building Morale: Keeping morale high in a virtual workplace can be challenging, but a Sales Team Lead can help by sharing regular feedback and recognition of great work done by their team members. They organize online team-building events and workshops to keep agents motivated towards achieving the established goals.

5. Leading by Example: Finally, the Sales Team Leader sets a precedent by actively leading from the front. They exemplify exceptional performance through excellent KPIs while demonstrating teamwork and effective communication skills with their agents. They set an example for the rest of their team to emulate, encouraging and instilling positive behaviors within teams.

In conclusion, setting goals and expectations that are specific, measurable, achievable, relevant, and time-bound is critical to achieving success in any remote call center. The Sales Team Leader plays a vital role in ensuring their team's success by prioritizing goal setting, clearly communicating expectations, continuously monitoring individual and team performance, fostering morale, and leading through example.

Chapter 3: Essential Communication & Interpersonal Skills

Essential Communication and Interpersonal Skills

Effective communication is essential for any sales team lead, especially in a remote call center environment. Without the ability to effectively communicate with team members and clients, the entire operation can be negatively impacted. As such, it is crucial that sales team leads possess strong verbal and written communication skills. Additionally, they must be skilled at active listening and adept at providing clear instructions, feedback, and guidance to their team.

In addition to effective communication skills, sales team leads also need strong interpersonal skills to successfully manage and motivate their team. Building relationships with team members is key to establishing trust and mutual respect. This can be particularly challenging in a remote call center setting where there are limited opportunities for in-person interactions. As such, successful sales team leads must be proactive in seeking out opportunities to connect with their team on a personal level while maintaining a professional relationship.

To ensure success as a sales team lead in a remote call center, it is also important to have a well-developed understanding of cultural differences and nuances. In a global economy where companies operate across borders and languages, it is crucial to have an appreciation for how cultural differences can impact communication and decision-making processes. Sales team leads who can navigate these issues with tact and sensitivity have a distinct advantage in building relationships and closing deals with customers from diverse backgrounds.

Active Listening and Empathy

Active listening and empathy are crucial skills for any Sales Team Lead, especially in a remote call center environment. Firstly, active listening allows team leads to truly understand what their team members are saying, enabling them to identify and address any issues or concerns they may have. This helps to build trust and rapport with the team, leading to better communication and ultimately, improved performance.

Empathy is important because it allows Sales Team Leads to put themselves in their team member's shoes and understand their perspective. By doing so, they can provide support and guidance that is tailored to everyone's needs, helping them to feel valued and supported. In a remote environment where team members may be feeling isolated or disconnected, this can make all the difference.

Effective active listening and empathetic communication can lead to greater synergy within the team. When team members feel heard and understood, they are more likely to collaborate and work together towards achieving common goals. This not only improves productivity but also creates a positive culture within the team and fosters long-term engagement and commitment

Additionally, active listening and empathy are critical for building strong relationships with customers. Sales Team Leads who can listen actively to customer needs and show empathy towards their challenges will be able to build rapport and trust quickly, helping to establish long-term relationships that drive repeat business.

Finally, active listening and empathy are important leadership qualities that set Sales Team Leads apart from their peers. By demonstrating these skills consistently, they can inspire their team members to do the same, creating a culture of empathy and active listening throughout the organization. As a result, teams are more likely to work collaboratively towards shared goals, leading to increased organizational success.

Conflict Resolution and Problem-solving

Conflict resolution and problem-solving are crucial skills for a Sales Team Lead in a remote call center because they have a direct impact on customer satisfaction, team morale, and ultimately, sales performance.

Primarily, conflict resolution is important for a Sales Team Lead in a remote call center as they are responsible for managing customer complaints or queries that may arise during the sales process. A Sales Team Lead with strong conflict resolution skills can calmly de-escalate tense situations and find mutually beneficial solutions. This leads to higher customer satisfaction and retention rates, ultimately driving sales growth.

Effective problem-solving skills are essential in a remote call center environment where immediate support from colleagues or managers may not always be possible. With excellent problem-solving skills, a Sales Team Lead can quickly identify issues, prioritize tasks and make informed decisions, ensuring sales processes run smoothly even under challenging circumstances.

Sales Team Leads in remote call centers often face communication barriers due to geographic and cultural differences. Conflict resolution skills help break down these barriers, promoting clearer communication channels and improving understanding between team members, resulting in improved trust and collaboration.

High levels of stress can be common in a fast-paced sales environment. Conflict resolution and problem-solving skills help Sales Team Leads manage stress both for themselves and amongst their teams. When individuals feel supported, conflicts are resolved effectively, and expectations are clearly communicated concerning deadlines, workload and objectives – stress levels can be minimized, leading to increased productivity and motivation.

Conflict resolution and problem-solving skills play a significant role in fostering a positive company culture. A Sales Team Lead who can model effective resolution of disputes motivates teams by creating an open-minded and inclusive work environment. A positive company culture promotes teamwork through active listening, respectful communication and clear goal setting - this translates to higher job satisfaction rates and employee retention.

In conclusion, Conflict resolution and problem-solving skills are crucial traits of an adept Sales Team Lead working in a remote call center. These skills help to de-escalate and resolve conflicts that arise in the sales process quickly, effectively prioritize tasks leading increased productivity, reduce stress levels for team members, improve communication channels, and foster a positive company culture that results in higher job satisfaction rates and employee retention – all of which positively impact team morale, customer satisfaction and ultimately drive sales growth.

Providing Clear and Constructive Feedback

Providing clear and constructive feedback is crucial for the role of a Sales Team Lead in a remote call center. The following are five key reasons why:

1. Improving Performance: Clear and constructive feedback can motivate sales agents to improve their performance by identifying areas that require attention. This approach encourages the team to work on enhancing their skills, knowledge, and customer service techniques. With regular feedback sessions, Sales Team Leads can impart best practices that have worked for others, share tips and tricks, and provide specific recommendations that align with the sales goals of both the individual and the organization.

2. Boosting Morale: Sales agents working remotely may feel disconnected from the team, leading to decreased morale. A Team Lead must ensure that every agent feels valued and supported, which helps to foster a positive working environment where ideas can be shared, and support can be offered. Regular feedback sessions increase communication between leaders and their teams, fostering teamwork, enhancing morale, and reinforcing the importance of maintaining high levels of engagement with customers.

3. Fostering Employee Growth: Providing feedback on strengths and weaknesses enables sales agents to grow both professionally and personally. By communicating an agent's progress towards goals and objectives or pointing out gaps in their understanding of internal processes, sales leaders can help promote employee development through personalized training opportunities.

4. Enhancing Customer Experience: Clear and constructive feedback can highlight areas where agents excel or fall short in providing customer service excellence. Addressing these shortcomings allows agents to make targeted improvements that directly impact the satisfaction of the customer. Promoting effective customer service not only makes the company more attractive to customers but also helps reinforce positive relationships between team members.

5. Increasing Company Success: Finally, all these benefits come together to help achieve company success. When employees are motivated, customer service improves, and productivity increases. As a result, Sales Team Leads will see more positive results, increasing revenue streams as well as building trust among clients and fostering a healthy company culture that contributes to long-term organizational growth.

Chapter 4: Motivating and Engaging Your Team

Motivating & Engaging Your Team

As a call center manager, it's your job to make sure your team is motivated and engaged. This can be a challenge, especially when your team is working remotely. But it's important to remember that motivation and engagement are key to productivity and performance. So how can you motivate and engage your team?

One way to do this is to set and celebrate milestones. This could be something as simple as celebrating the completion of a project or the achievement of a goal. Celebrating milestones helps your team feel appreciated and recognized for their hard work.

Another way to motivate and engage your team is to offer incentives and rewards. This could be something like offering a bonus for meeting a certain target or providing extra time off for employees who go above and beyond. Incentives and rewards can be a great way to motivate your team to work hard and achieve their goals.

Finally, you can encourage teamwork and collaboration by setting up team-building activities and events. This could be something as simple as having a team lunch once a month or setting up a team-wide volunteer day. By encouraging teamwork and collaboration, you can create a sense of camaraderie and unity among your team.

Setting Goals and Celebrating Milestones

One of the key responsibilities of a sales team lead in a remote call center is to set and celebrate milestones for their agents. Here are five paragraphs on how they can do so effectively:

Setting Goals: The first step to celebrating milestones is setting attainable goals for each agent. This not only motivates them but also provides the leader with specific targets for evaluating performance. A Sales Team Lead should set ambitious, yet achievable monthly or quarterly goals that are aligned with the organization's vision.

Tracking Progress: As a Team Leader, it is crucial to have access to data that tracks individual progress of the agents against their goals at any given time.

23

This allows them to intervene proactively if there is a danger of an agent not meeting their target, and promptly recognize an agent who exceeded their goal.

Celebrate Individual Achievements: Every achievement, no matter how small, should be recognized and celebrated by the Team Leader. Meaningful recognition helps reinforce positive behavior and create a culture of success. Celebrations can happen via group messages, video calls or email recognitions like shout outs publicly shared across the company.

Celebrate Team Efforts: Good sales performances always involve teamwork, encouraging esprit de corps in Agents benefits both individual morale and overall team production. In addition to celebrating individual achievements, Leaders should also acknowledge collective successes through team-based incentives, consistent peer-to-peer recognition, and regular acknowledgments in company-wide meetings.

Collaborate to improve: Milestones evaluations shouldn't be something one side does, leaders should gather feedback from their team members on metrics measuring key performance indicators (KPIs). As with celebrations, it is essential to involve everyone in this process ensuring transparent communication throughout the team. Finding ways to support those that need help improves everyone's collective chances of success.

Incentives and Rewards

A sales team lead plays a critical role in motivating and encouraging their agents to achieve their targets, especially in a remote call center. One effective way to achieve this is by implementing a robust incentives and rewards program that recognizes exceptional performance and promotes healthy competition amongst the team.

Goals and Objectives: The first step in designing an effective incentives and rewards program is to set clear goals and objectives. This includes identifying key performance indicators such as sales targets, customer satisfaction ratings, and call quality scores that will be used to evaluate the success of the program. By having these metrics in place, both managers and agents can work towards these objectives with tangible rewards in sight.

Types of Incentives: Incentives can come in various forms, but some of the most common ways to motivate and reward agents include cash bonuses, gift cards, extra time off, and personalized company swag. Sales contests are another popular form of incentive where top-performing agents are recognized with prizes like a weekend getaway or tickets to a sporting event. To maximize effectiveness, incentives should be tailored to your remote sales team's preferences, including location and demographics.

Communication and Transparency: It's crucial to ensure that incentives and rewards programs are communicated clearly to all members of the sales team regularly. By outlining the parameters for qualifying for specific incentives or rewards, the entire team is clued into what they need to do to hit their targets. Transparency is also essential when it comes to tracking results so that each agent can see where they stack up against their peers.

Evaluation and Feedback: Lastly, it's crucial to evaluate the effectiveness of your incentives and rewards program regularly. Collecting feedback from your agents through surveys or one-on-one meetings can help you identify any concerns or areas that need improvement. This input is valuable in shaping and refining your incentives and rewards program to ensure its ongoing effectiveness in motivating your sales team.

Overall, implementing the right incentives and rewards program is a powerful tool to keep your remote call center's performance at optimal levels. Providing incentives helps maintain an engaged and motivated remote team that understands and sees a tangible reward for meeting or exceeding their targets.

Encouraging Teamwork and Collaboration

Teamwork and collaboration are essential for success in a remote call center, where agents work independently but need to coordinate efforts to meet team goals. Here are five ways a Sales Team Lead can encourage teamwork and collaboration among their agents:

Establish clear communication channels - Effective communication is crucial in a remote call center, and the Sales Team Lead should ensure that all agents have access to the necessary communication tools such as video conferencing, messaging apps, and email. They should also schedule regular team meetings and individual check-ins to build a sense of camaraderie and give agents an opportunity to share feedback.

Foster a positive team culture - The Sales Team Lead can build a sense of community by creating engaging virtual team building activities like online quizzes, games, or contests. Encouraging social conversations helps to create emotional connections among the agents, which makes it easier for them to collaborate effectively later.

Promote cross-departmental engagement - Remote call centers function best when different departments work together effectively. The Sales Team Lead can organize joint training sessions with support staff or quality assurance teams to explain the value of collaborating across departments and provide opportunities for brainstorming solutions.

Provide encouragement and recognition - A Sales Team Lead should recognize that performance in a remote context can be challenging, and frequent positive reinforcement can go a long way. Acknowledge achievements both on an individual and group level, consider providing incentives such as bonuses or time off as a reward for meeting targets or deadlines, and highlight successful collaboration efforts.

Encourage knowledge sharing - Agents can learn from one another's strategies, tactics, and successes. The Sales Team Lead could set up a "knowledge sharing" platform where reps could post ideas, they've found helpful, document their experiences, and share tips for working more efficiently. Team members should be encouraged to participate in discussions and provide feedback on each other's posts, which will foster innovation within the team while also promoting collaboration.

In sum, a Sales Team Lead can encourage teamwork and collaboration by establishing clear communication channels, fostering a positive team culture, promoting cross-departmental engagement, providing encouragement and recognition and encouraging knowledge sharing among the agents.

Chapter 5: Sales Coaching and Performance Management

Sales Coaching and Performance Management

The role of a sales team lead in a remote call center is critical to the success of the sales team. As a sales team lead, you are responsible for managing a group of sales representatives who are working from different locations. Your job is not just to ensure that your team meets their sales targets, but it's also about coaching and helping them improve their skills, performance, and productivity while working remotely.

One of the keyways to coach and manage the performance of your remote sales team is by providing regular feedback. Unlike in-person communication, remote work can make it more challenging to gauge how well your team members are performing. By offering constant feedback, you can help your team identify areas for improvement and build on their strengths to achieve better results. Feedback should be specific, actionable, and timely.

Another important aspect of coaching and performance management for remote sales teams is training. Remote sales reps may face unique challenges, such as technical difficulties, time zone differences, or distractions at home. Providing comprehensive training that covers these issues will help your team overcome these challenges and perform better. You can offer virtual training sessions through video conferencing or create self-paced learning modules that your team can access anytime and anywhere.

As a sales team lead, it's crucial to set clear expectations and goals for your sales reps. When everyone on your team understands what they need to achieve and how their performance is being measured, they are more likely to stay motivated and on track. Be sure to communicate these expectations regularly and hold periodic check-ins to review progress toward goals.

Lastly, one of the most effective ways to coach and manage the performance of your remote sales team is by using data-driven insights. Tracking key metrics like call-to-sale ratios or conversion rates can give you valuable insights into what's working and what's not. Unfortunately, it can be challenging to access data across many remote locations. Invest in a reporting system that collects data from all locations, or even consider using performance management software that can generate reports in real-time based on pre-defined metrics. This will enable you to make informed decisions about how to improve the performance of your remote sales team.

Identifying Strengths & Areas of Improvement

Use call analytics: Analyze agents' calls using call analytics software to identify areas where they excel, such as effective communication, problem-solving, or product knowledge. Identify areas that need improvement, such as tone of voice, length of time on calls, or missing important information.

Conduct one-on-one assessments: Schedule time with each agent for a one-on-one discussion to evaluate their performance. Ask them about their challenges, strengths, and weaknesses. Use this information to create a plan for improvement.

Monitor performance metrics: Use key performance indicators (KPIs) to track your team's performance regularly. This will help you assess individual performance against team goals and identify areas where improvements need to be made.

Review customer feedback: Check customer reviews and ratings data to get a sense of how well agents are performing in terms of customer satisfaction. Look for patterns in complaints or praise to identify areas of weakness or strength.

Use coaching and training programs: Offer coaching and training opportunities tailored to the specific needs of each team member. Provide them with constructive criticism and resources that focus on their development areas, which can include communication, sales techniques or product knowledge. Continuous learning and support will help enhance the agents' skills and improve performance over time.

Providing Targeted Coaching & Support

Establish Clear Expectations: A sales team lead should first establish clear expectations for their agents and clearly outline the key performance indicators that they will be held accountable for. In a remote call center, it's important to communicate these expectations regularly and provide ongoing feedback to ensure agents are meeting their targets.

Implement Coaching & Training Programs: To support their agents, a sales team lead should implement coaching and training programs that are designed to help agents acquire the skills they need to perform at a high level. These programs can include virtual training sessions, e-learning modules, and one-on-one coaching sessions.

Utilize Technology: Technology is critical in a remote call center environment. Sales team leads can use various tools and technologies to provide targeted coaching and support to their agents. For example, screen sharing tools can be used to observe and coach agents as they interact with customers.

Provide Regular Feedback & Recognition: A remote call center environment can be isolating for agents, so regular feedback and recognition from their sales team lead can go a long way in keeping them motivated and engaged. This can take the form of individualized feedback on specific calls or emails, or public recognition for achieving goals or milestones.

Emphasize Collaboration & Teamwork: Finally, a sales team lead should emphasize collaboration and teamwork among their agents. By establishing a strong sense of community within the team, agents will feel more connected to each other and the company. This can improve morale, encourage knowledge-sharing, and foster a sense of accountability among team members.

Conducting Regular Performance Reviews

Conduct Regular One-on-One Meetings: As a sales team lead, it is important to conduct regular one-on-one meetings with your agents in a remote call center. These meetings should be structured and include a review of the agent's performance over the past few weeks or months. This will help you identify areas where they are excelling and areas where they need to improve. Take a moment out of your day to simply check-in with each agent, even if it is just to say, "Good morning."

Set Clear Expectations and Goals: During these meetings, set clear expectations and goals for each agent. Be specific about what you expect from them and set targets that are achievable yet challenging. This will enable them to focus on their work and measure their progress over time.

Provide Constructive Feedback: Performance reviews are an excellent opportunity to provide constructive feedback to your agents. Be honest with them about their strengths and weaknesses and offer suggestions on how they can improve their performance. Make sure to highlight their successes as well and acknowledge any improvements they have made since the last review.

Use Metrics to Measure Performance: In a remote call center, it can be challenging to measure the performance of agents. However, by using metrics such as call volume, customer satisfaction scores, and sales numbers, you can track how each agent is performing. This information can be used during performance reviews to identify areas where improvement is needed.

Create Action Plans: After conducting performance reviews, create action plans for each agent based on the feedback provided. These plans should outline specific actions that agents can take to improve their performance, such as attending training sessions, improving their communication skills, or focusing on meeting specific targets. By creating action plans, you can ensure that your agents are aware of what they need to do to improve and that they have a roadmap for achieving their goals. Overall, regular performance reviews in a remote call center led to more engaged employees who are aware of their strengths and weaknesses and motivated to improve their performance, which translates into higher sales and customer satisfaction.

In summary, effective performance management requires ongoing assessment and feedback. Managers need to identify the key strengths and weaknesses of their employees, as well as opportunities for growth. With a clear understanding of performance gaps, managers can then provide targeted coaching and support to help employees improve and develop their skills.

Regular performance reviews, whether formal or informal, give managers a chance to review progress, discuss achievements and challenges, and re-align goals and development plans. When performance reviews are constructive, transparent, and focused on behavior and results rather than personal traits, they can be a tool for enhancing motivation, engagement and productivity.

By continuously identifying strengths and weaknesses, providing tailored coaching, and conducting thoughtful performance reviews, managers can effectively manage performance and help their employees reach their full potential. Employees will appreciate the feedback and guidance and will be better equipped to exceed expectations and contribute at a high level.

In short, performance management is about ongoing development, not just annual reviews. With the right approach, managers can turn performance management into a strategic process that benefits both individuals and organizations.

Chapter 6: Effective Call Center Metrics and KPIs

Effective Call Center Metrics and KPIs

Measurement is key to understanding business performance and enhancing operations efficiency. For call centers, establishing and monitoring meaningful metrics and key performance indicators (KPIs) are critical to evaluating agent productivity, customer experience, and overall services quality.

This chapter explores the topic of effective call center metrics and KPIs. It begins by discussing some of the most useful metrics for call centers including average call duration, handle time, service level, and agent occupancy. Choosing metrics that matter and align to business objectives is essential.

Next, the chapter examines how to analyze and interpret the metrics to uncover opportunities for improvement and gain valuable insights. By detecting trends, comparing metrics across teams and time periods, and benchmarking against industry standards, call centers can determine what is and is not working.

Using metrics to drive improvement and change is one of the key benefits of a data-driven organization. Several examples of how call centers have leveraged metrics to optimize processes, enhance agent effectiveness, and strengthen customer relationships will be presented.

In summary, this chapter provides a framework and guidance for selecting, measuring, and taking action on the metrics that matter most for call center operations and services. With the right metrics in place and a commitment to metric-driven management, call centers can achieve and surpass key business goals.

Selecting the Right Metrics

To gain a better understanding, we will explore how a Sales Team Lead can select the right metrics in a remote call center to measure the performance of their team accurately. With the rise of remote work, it's essential that Sales Team Leads are equipped with the tools to monitor and analyze their teams' performance remotely. We'll discuss why measuring the right metrics is critical and outline some best practices for selecting metrics.

The first step in selecting the right metrics is to understand the goals and objectives of your remote call center team. Are you looking to increase sales, improve customer satisfaction, or reduce churn rate? Once you have determined these objectives, you can identify relevant key performance indicators (KPIs) in line with them. For example, if boosting sales is your primary goal, conversion rates, average deal size, and outbound call rates could be KPIs that you track.

After identifying relevant KPIs, the next step is to ensure they are measurable using the tools available in your remote call center environment. Many remote call center platforms offer features such as call recording functions or real-time monitoring dashboards that can help measure KPIs accurately. Be sure to assess which tools align with your team's needs while keeping budget and workforce capacity in mind.

A good metric should also be timely, easily communicable, and actionable. Consider setting up a system to collect data at specific intervals so that you can quickly identify swings in performance that require attention in time. Use visual aids such as graphs or charts to communicate results easily to your team. Finally, create action plans aligned with your KPIs to drive better performance.

It's also important to remember that not all KPIs have equal importance. Rather than tracking too many KPIs, focus on a select few that are most critical to your team's goals. Additionally, some metrics must be analyzed as a part of a broader context, such as industry benchmarks or current market trends, to provide more insight and context.

In conclusion, selecting the right metrics is crucial for managing remote call center sales teams effectively. After identifying relevant KPIs that align with your team's goals, ensuring they are actionable, measurable, timely, and focus on creating a system for effective tracking, communication, analysis and action plan can improve performance. Remember that this will be an ongoing process, so regularly assess the outcome through reviewing data and tweaking strategies, including metric boundaries.

Analyzing and Interpreting Data

As a Sales Team Lead in a remote call center, analyzing and interpreting data is essential to achieving sustainable sales growth. The process begins with defining the key performance indicators (KPIs) that are most important for the team's success. This can include metrics such as conversion rates, average handling times, and customer satisfaction scores.

Once these KPIs have been established, the next step is to regularly track and monitor them using tools like dashboards and reports. Analyzing this data provides insights into how the team is performing against their goals and where they need to improve.

Interpreting this data requires a combination of quantitative and qualitative analysis. Looking at raw numbers without context can be misleading, so it's important to gather additional information from sources like customer feedback or individual agent performance reviews.

Using this information, sales team leads can identify trends, patterns, and areas where performance can be improved. By sharing these insights with the team and providing actionable feedback, they can work collaboratively towards achieving their shared goals.

Ultimately, effective data analysis and interpretation is crucial for any sales team lead in a remote call center. By understanding the metrics that matter most and using insights to drive improvement, they can help their team achieve sustainable growth and success in a challenging and competitive environment.

Using Metric to Drive Improvement

As a Sales Team Lead of a remote call center, metrics are critical to driving improvement and performance. By analyzing key metrics such as average handle time, sales per call, call quality scores, and agent productivity, opportunities for improvement can be identified. Regular review and discussion of these metrics with the sales team lead to targeted actions to improve metrics.

One of the most important metrics is average handle time (AHT). AHT measures the average time each call is engaged, which impacts how many calls can be handled. If AHT is too high, not enough calls are being handled to meet sales targets. Work with agents to find ways to shorten AHT such as through improved first call resolution, sales process efficiency, and limiting non-essential conversations with customers. Set goals and incentives to motivate agents to lower AHT.

Sales per call and call quality scores also provide insight into agent effectiveness and opportunities. Identify any agents with consistently low sales per call or quality scores and determine if additional coaching, mentoring or skills development is needed. Plan with the agents to improve their metrics through better targeting high potential leads, focusing on key messaging, and asking more questions to uncover customer needs. Monitor metrics to ensure improvements are being made.

Scaled metrics, such as total calls answered and sales dollars per agent, give an overall view of the productivity and performance of the entire team. Set targets for productivity, sales volume, and other key metrics. Develop strategies to provide more high-potential leads and customer referrals to agents or modify the agent assignment model to ensure the team is optimized. Make changes to schedules, rosters or shifts as needed to reach scaled metrics.

In summary, as a Sales Team Lead of a remote call center, regularly reviewing and analyzing metrics is essential to improving agent and team performance. By identifying the root causes of subpar metrics and creating targeted plans to address issues, meaningful and sustainable performance improvements can be achieved. Continuous monitoring and optimization of metrics will keep the sales team progressing toward success.

Chapter 7: Time Management and Prioritization for Team Leaders

Time Management and Prioritization for Team Leaders

Effective time management and prioritization are crucial skills for any team leader striving to achieve success. As a team leader, your ability to set priorities and goals will have a direct impact on the productivity and effectiveness of your team. Delegating tasks effectively is also an essential component of time management, as it allows you to focus on the most important items on your own to-do list while ensuring that other tasks are being accomplished by appropriate individuals. Balancing individual and team responsibilities is yet another challenge faced by team leaders when managing time. Mastering these skills requires discipline, organization, and effective communication.

Setting priorities and goals is at the core of effective time management. By determining what tasks are most urgent or important, you can allocate your resources, accordingly, making sure that the most critical tasks are completed first. Establishing clear and measurable goals can also help maintain focus and provide direction for both you and your team.

Delegating tasks effectively is another critical skill for team leaders as it enables the efficient distribution of responsibilities among team members based on their strengths and weaknesses. This can be done through effective communication, establishing clear expectations, and providing adequate training and support. Effective delegation frees up valuable time for leaders to work on high-priority tasks while ensuring the smooth operation of the team.

Balancing individual and team responsibilities is essential for achieving optimal performance levels. Great leaders understand the importance of fostering a strong sense of teamwork while still providing individual accountability. Encouraging collaboration among team members while respecting each member's personal goals and motivations plays an important role in creating a productive and harmonious work environment.

In conclusion, mastering time management and prioritization skills is vital for success in any leadership role. Team leaders who prioritize setting goals, delegating tasks effectively, and balancing individual and team responsibilities will enable their teams to work cohesively towards shared objectives. With practice, perseverance, and a willingness to learn, anyone can become an effective team leader proficient at managing time and achieving their goals.

Setting Priorities and Goals

Effective sales team leadership involves setting priorities and goals for agents to achieve organizational objectives, especially in remote call center settings where virtual collaboration and communication are crucial. Here are five essential steps a sales team lead can take to set priorities and goals and enhance overall team performance in a remote environment:

Establish clear expectations: Start by defining the objectives that your remote team should accomplish, such as specific targets for calls handled, leads generated, or conversions made. Communicate these expectations explicitly and clearly, emphasizing the importance of achieving them and how they contribute to the company's success. Be sure to include metrics that you'll use to track their progress and how often you'll be checking in. Encourage open communication: Foster a sense of teamwork, encourage collaboration, and ensure team members understand that their input is valued. Regular check-ins with the group about individual goal setting and progress toward collective objectives can help maintain focus, accountability, and promote discussion on any barriers preventing them from reaching their goals.

Develop personal plans: Collaborate with each team member to develop personal goals that align with wider organizational goals. Work together to determine the best course of action for meeting these goals, offering practical advice, access to training materials, and encouragement along the way.

Provide feedback and recognition: Give your team members feedback that both acknowledges their successes and offers constructive criticism for areas requiring improvement in real-time. Celebrating small achievements, such as when someone meets a particular target, provides a critical boost that encourages team members to keep working hard.

Evaluate and prioritize regularly: Sales team leadership is an ongoing process, so it's essential to evaluate regularly and realign objectives accordingly. Prioritize accordingly based on feedback, changing markets, or emerging challenges. This involves adjusting internal benchmarks if factors impacting performance change, outlining new targets within quarterly or monthly updates, leading your team through brainstorming sessions for new ways to exceed existing targets.

By setting realistic objectives and clarifying expectations, communicating regularly with the team, offering support and timely feedback, and reviewing progress regularly, a sales team lead can improve chances of success for both individuals and the team. No matter where your team is located, these steps will ensure that everyone remains focused, engaged and energized to succeed.

Delegating Tasks Effectively

Effective delegation is a crucial skill for sales team leads, particularly in remote call centers. It enables team members to take ownership of their work and feel valued while allowing leaders to focus on high-level strategy. Here are five ways that sales team leads can delegate tasks effectively in a remote call center and improve overall performance:

Clearly define roles and responsibilities: Start by outlining each team member's job description, so everyone knows what they should be working on. Set clear expectations, deadlines, and deliverables for each role to avoid confusion.

Use collaboration tools: Utilize project management and communication tools like Asana, Trello, or Slack to keep track of assignments, progress, and deadlines. These tools will help teammates stay on the same page and allow leaders to see how well projects are progressing.

Empower team members: Give team members autonomy over the work you assign them. Listen to their ideas and feedback, encourage them to come up with solutions, and help when needed. When team members feel empowered, they become more invested in the work they're doing.

Provide support: Ensure all team members have access to the resources they need to complete their tasks effectively. Monitor performance regularly and be available to guide team members and give feedback as required.

Celebrate successes: When a project is completed successfully, recognize and celebrate it with your team. Recognition motivates employees and empowers them to do better in the future.

In conclusion, delegating tasks effectively can make a significant impact on the performance of a remote sales call center team. By clearly defining roles and responsibilities, using collaboration tools, empowering team members, providing support, and celebrating successes, sales team leads can create an environment that fosters productivity, creativity, and agility while simultaneously building a sense of teamwork and accountability among team members.

Balancing Individual and Team Responsibilities

As the sales team lead, you must balance your individual responsibilities with your team's collective goals. This can be a challenge in a remote call center, where you may not have the opportunity to interact with your team members face-to-face. However, there are several ways to improve overall performance while balancing individual and team responsibilities.

You should regularly check in with your team members to see how they are doing and to provide any support they may need. This can be done through regular one-on-one meetings or team meetings. During these meetings, you should discuss individual goals and progress, as well as any challenges or concerns team members may have. You should also use these meetings to provide feedback and coaching to help team members improve their performance.

Next, you should also work to create a culture of accountability within your team. This means setting clear goals and expectations for team members and holding them accountable for their performance. You should also provide regular feedback and recognition to team members to help them feel valued and motivated.

Then, you should encourage team members to collaborate and share ideas with each other. This can be done through team meetings or online collaboration tools. By encouraging collaboration, you can help team members learn from each other and improve their overall performance.

Finally, you should also work to create a sense of community within your team. This can be done through team-building activities or social events. By creating a sense of community, you can help team members feel more connected and motivated to work together towards common goals. Overall, balancing individual and team responsibilities in a remote call center can be a challenge. However, by regularly checking in with team members, creating a culture of accountability, encouraging collaboration, and building a sense of community, you can help improve overall performance.

Chapter 8: Sales Strategies and Techniques for Call Center Success

Sales Strategies and Techniques for Call Center Success

As a team lead in a call center, you are responsible for achieving sales targets and coaching your agents to perform at their best. To succeed in this role, you need a solid understanding of sales strategies and techniques that work in your industry and for your customers. In this chapter, we will cover three key aspects of call center selling: developing a sales script, handling objections and closing deals, and utilizing technology and tools to improve performance.

Developing a sales script is a critical step in creating a consistent and persuasive message that resonates with your target audience. Your script should reflect the needs and preferences of your customers, as well as the benefits and features of your product or service. Good sales script also allows for customization and personalization, so that each agent can adapt it to the specific situation and customer they are talking to. We'll explore examples of effective call center scripts and provide tips on how to create one that works for your team.

Handling objections and closing deals are the two skills that separate successful salespeople from average ones. Objections are a natural part of selling, but they can also be opportunities to address concerns and build trust with the customer. By learning how to handle common objections and offer compelling responses, your agents can increase their success rate and improve customer satisfaction. Closing deals requires persistence, confidence, and a willingness to ask for the sale. We'll discuss different closing techniques that can help your team close more deals without sounding pushy or desperate.

Utilizing technology and tools is another way to enhance the effectiveness of your call center sales team. From CRM software to predictive dialers, there are many solutions available that can streamline your workflows, track your metrics, and identify areas for improvement. However, not all technology is created equal, and not all tools are suitable for every situation. We'll review the most important criteria to consider when selecting and implementing technology and tools in your call center.

In conclusion, mastering sales strategies and techniques is essential for any team lead who wants to achieve call center success. By developing a strong sales script, handling objections and closing deals effectively, and utilizing technology and tools wisely, your team can improve their performance and exceed their targets. In the following sections, we'll dive deeper into each of these topics and provide practical advice and examples that you can apply immediately.

Developing a Sales Script

Developing an effective sales script can greatly improve the performance of a sales team lead in a remote call center. Here are five paragraphs on how to do it.

Understand Your Audience: Before writing any sales script, it's important to understand who your audience is. This includes knowing their demographics, pain points, and motivations for making a purchase. This information can be gathered through market research, customer feedback, and analyzing past sales data. With this knowledge, you can craft a personalized script that resonates with their needs.

Highlight the Benefits: The most effective sales scripts focus on highlighting the benefits of the product or service being sold. Rather than just describing features, emphasize how these features can solve the customer's pain points or improve their life. Use persuasive language that encourages the customer to envision themselves using the product and enjoying its benefits.

Keep it Simple: In a remote call center environment where communication can be challenging, it's important to keep the sales script simple and concise. Avoid technical jargon and rely on layman's terms that the customer will understand easily. A clear and straightforward message is more likely to resonate with customers than a convoluted one.

Encourage Customer Engagement: An effective sales script should encourage customer engagement through open-ended questions and active listening. Instead of talking at the customer, involve them in the conversation by asking questions that elicit valuable information about their needs and preferences. Listening actively also allows the sales team lead to address any objections the customer might have and respond appropriately.

Continuously Adapt and Improve: Finally, no sales script is perfect, and there is always room for improvement. Sales team leads should regularly collect feedback from customers and monitor key performance indicators (KPIs) such as conversion rates and average call times to identify areas that need improvement. Based on this feedback, the script can be tweaked and refined to better meet the needs of customers and improve overall performance.

Handling Objections & Closing Deals

Sales team leads play a crucial role in helping agents handle objections and close sales on the phone in remote call centers. Here are five ways they can provide support:

Training and coaching: Sales team leads can provide extensive training and coaching to agents on how to handle objections effectively. They can develop custom objection handling scripts that align with the product or service they are selling, coach agents on their tone and approach, and share best practices for closing sales on the phone.

Monitoring calls: Sales team leads should monitor the calls of their agents to identify areas where they struggle with handling objections or closing sales. This allows them to provide timely feedback to agents on how they can improve.

Providing real-time support: During live calls, sales team leads can offer immediate assistance to agents if they encounter any unexpected objections. This can involve providing additional information about the product or service being sold or suggesting alternative approaches for handling the objection.

Motivating agents: Sales team leads can motivate agents to stay focused and engaged by setting achievable targets, offering incentives for meeting objectives, and recognizing their achievements publicly. This encourages agents to be proactive in their approach to handling objections and closing sales.

Analyzing data: Sales team leads should analyze data from successful and unsuccessful sales calls to identify trends, patterns, and common objections. This information can then be used to create targeted training programs, refine objection handling scripts, and continually improve the sales process.

Utilizing Technology and Tools

With the rise of remote work and the increasing use of technology and tools in call centers, sales team leaders are responsible for developing sales strategies that take advantage of these changes. Here are some ways that sales team leaders can develop effective sales strategies in a remote call center environment:

Use technology and tools to improve communication and collaboration: With the use of technology and tools such as chat, video conferencing, and shared documents, sales team leaders can improve communication and collaboration with their team members. This can help to improve the effectiveness of sales strategies by allowing team members to share ideas and feedback more easily.

Leverage data and analytics to track performance and identify opportunities: With the increasing use of technology and tools in call centers, sales team leaders have access to more data and analytics than ever before. By leveraging this data, sales team leaders can track the performance of their team members and identify opportunities for improvement.

Use technology and tools to improve efficiency: With the use of technology and tools, sales team leaders can improve the efficiency of their team members. For example, using a customer relationship management (CRM) system can help team members to track leads and sales opportunities more effectively.

Leverage technology and tools to improve the customer experience: With the use of technology and tools, sales team leaders can improve the customer experience. For example, using a chatbot can help to quickly and easily answer customer questions, while using a video conferencing tool can allow team members to provide more personalized service to customers.

Use technology and tools to stay up to date on industry trends: With the increasing use of technology and tools in call centers, it is important for sales team leaders to stay up to date on industry trends. By using technology and tools to stay informed, sales team leaders can ensure that their team members are using the most effective sales strategies. Overall, by leveraging technology and tools in a remote call center environment, sales team leaders can develop effective sales strategies that take advantage of these changes.

Chapter 9: Navigating and Managing Change in a Call Center

Navigating & Managing Change in a Call Center

Change is inevitable, especially in today's dynamic business environment. In this chapter, we'll explore how to navigate and manage change in the context of a remote sales call center. We'll discuss three key aspects of change management: identifying and addressing resistance to change, communicating change effectively, and implementing and evaluating change initiatives.

We need to recognize that some employees might be resistant to change. It could be due to fear of the unknown, job insecurity, or personal comfort zones. To address resistance, we must proactively involve employees throughout the changes process. We should communicate the reasons for the change and its benefits, provide training on new processes and technologies, and soliciting feedback from our team.

Communication is vital when managing change in virtual environments. Clear and consistent messaging helps employees feel informed and included. Ensure early communication of any changes, document updates regularly, consider creating a virtual town hall meeting and have someone available to answer questions efficiently.

Implementing and evaluating the chosen change initiatives is key. A structured plan ensures that all stakeholders understand what is happening at each stage. Monitor progress towards goals frequently, collaborate with the larger team to spot red flags and make necessary adjustments as needed.

In conclusion, effective change management in remote sales call centers requires clear and consistent communication, teamwork between leadership and individual contributors, and diligent execution of planned initiatives across time. By focusing on these key areas, we can foster a culture of agility and adaptability that will drive success in today's ever-changing market.

Identifying and Addressing Resistance to Change

A sales team lead plays a pivotal role in identifying and addressing resistance to change in any sales environment. In a remote sales call center, this is especially important as team members may feel disconnected from one another and the organization. Here are five ways in which a sales team lead can assist with addressing resistance to change in a remote sales call center:

Communicating the need for change: A sales team lead should clearly communicate the reason behind the change to the team members. This will help them understand the importance of the change and how it will benefit both the organization and them.

Addressing concerns: Team members may have concerns or objections about the change. The sales team lead should address these concerns and help find solutions to any problems that may arise from the change.

Providing guidance: Change can be overwhelming, and team members may not know where to start or what is expected of them. The sales team lead should provide direction and guidance on how to implement the change effectively.

Encouraging participation: Employees who feel involved in the decision-making process are more likely to support the change. The sales team lead should encourage participation from all team members, providing opportunities for their input and feedback.

Monitoring progress: Even after the change has been implemented, some team members may still show resistance. The sales team lead should monitor progress and address any issues before they become major roadblocks. By keeping an open line of communication with team members, the sales team lead can ensure that everyone is on board with the change and working towards its successful implementation.

Communicating Change Effectively

Effective communication is key in any workplace, but it becomes even more important when trying to implement changes in the remote sales call center. Here are five ways sales team leads can communicate change effectively in a remote sales call center:

Set clear expectations: It is crucial to set clear expectations for your team members about the upcoming change, including how it will affect their roles and responsibilities. Sales team leads must provide a complete understanding of the reason for the change and the expected outcomes.

Hold regular meetings: To ensure that everyone is on the same page, hold regular meetings with your team, both one-on-one and as a group. These meetings should allow ample time for discussion and questions from your sales representatives.

Provide training & resources: Ensure that your sales reps receive adequate training and resources to support the change. This could include online tutorials, webinars, or informational videos.

Culture of transparency and feedback: Encourage open dialogue within your team by fostering an environment that values transparency and feedback. Sales team leads should be upfront about any challenges and areas where they need input from their team members.

Lead by example: Finally, lead by example by implementing the change yourself and demonstrating its value to your sales reps. Be engaged, energetic, and supportive throughout the process to show your team that you're invested in their success. Remember, actions speak louder than words.

Implementing & Evaluating Change

A sales team lead plays a crucial role in implementing and evaluating change initiatives in a remote sales call center. Here are five keyways that a sales team lead can assist with these efforts:

Communicating the vision: The sales team lead is responsible for communicating the vision of the change initiative to their team members. They should explain why this change is necessary, what it entails, and how it will benefit everyone involved. A clear and compelling vision helps to ensure buy-in from the sales team, which can make all the difference when it comes to implementing and sustaining changes.

Providing training and support: Implementing a change initiative often requires new skills or processes. The sales team lead can help by providing training and support to team members so they can adapt to the changes. This may involve scheduling regular training sessions or providing resources such as quick reference guides or online tutorials.

Setting expectations: Change can be disruptive, but setting clear expectations about what's changing and why is essential. Sales team leads should communicate these expectations, help their teams understand any new responsibilities or requirements, and provide ongoing feedback to help everyone stay on track.

Gathering data: It's important to track progress when implementing a change initiative. The sales team lead can assist by gathering data about how well the changes are working. This might include metrics such as customer satisfaction scores or sales figures. The data can then be used to evaluate whether the change initiative is achieving its objectives and inform any necessary tweaks or adjustments.

Celebrating successes: Finally, celebrating successes along the way is essential for keeping sales team members motivated and engaged in the process. When milestones are achieved, sales team leads should acknowledge and celebrate them to maintain momentum and keep everyone focused on the end goal. Whether it's a public shout-out during a team meeting or sending out celebratory

Chapter 10: Continuous Learning & Professional Development for Team Leaders

Continuous Learning & Professional Development for Team Leaders

Continuous learning and professional development are essential for effective team leaders. In this chapter, we explore three important practices that can help you grow both personally and professionally.

Identifying personal and professional growth opportunities is key to improving your skills as a leader. This involves being curious and open to new ideas, seeking out challenging assignments, and taking courses or attending workshops that align with your goals.

Seek feedback and mentorship from colleagues, superiors, and industry experts. Feedback can help you identify areas for improvement and build on your strengths, while mentorship can provide guidance and support as you navigate challenges and opportunities.

It is crucial to stay current with industry trends and best practices. Keep an eye on emerging technologies and changes in the marketplace, engage with thought leaders in your field and attend conferences or webinars to keep abreast of the latest developments.

By implementing these practices, team leaders can enhance their leadership abilities, develop new skills, and advance their careers. Continuous learning and professional development will enable you to adapt to changes in your industry, remain competitive, and lead your team effectively.

Identifying Personal & Professional Growth Opportunities

Embrace Continuous Learning: A sales team lead in a remote call center should strive to continuously learn and develop new skills. They can identify personal and professional growth opportunities by seeking out online courses, attending remote conferences or joining industry-related webinars.

Set SMART Goals: It is important for sales team leads to set specific, measurable, achievable, realistic, and time-bound goals. By setting goals aligned with their personal and professional growth objectives, they can identify areas of improvement and track progress through regular evaluation.

Seek Feedback: Soliciting feedback from colleagues, managers and clients is an excellent way for sales team leads to gain actionable insights on how they can improve their personal and professional skills. This feedback can help them to make necessary changes while also providing an opportunity to gauge their knowledge and experience.

Self-Assessment: Sales team leads should self-assess regularly to understand their strengths and weaknesses. This knowledge will enable them to identify where they need to grow professionally, such as learning a new software system or improving communication skills with the team or customers.

Mentorship: Sales team leads can seek mentorship from experienced professionals in their field to gain knowledge and guidance from persons with more experience. Mentors can serve as sounding boards for ideas, provide industry insights, and offer support in challenging situations. They can also help sales team leads identify areas where they can improve and provide advice on how to overcome these challenges.

Seek Feedback and Mentorship

As a Sales Team Lead in a remote call center, seeking feedback and mentorship can be challenging. However, here are five ways to effectively seek feedback and mentorship:

Schedule one-on-one virtual meetings with senior leaders: Arrange virtual meetings with senior leaders who have vast experience within the sales industry. During these meetings, share the team's progress, present any challenges faced by team members, and request for feedback on strategies that would drive sales.

Set up regular team huddles: Encourage regular team huddles where your team can brainstorm ideas, discuss the areas they need improvement or seek clarification from you or more experienced team members.

Online Community/Network Group: Join an online community or network group (e.g., LinkedIn Groups) where you can connect with other sales experts working remotely. Share best practices and solicit feedback on specific questions or topics to improve performance.

Attend virtual training courses: Participating in virtual training courses is a great way to gain new insights in the sales industry and connect with experts. Take advantage of online sales training sessions, conferences or webinars to enrich your knowledge, refine your skills and continuously learn and grow.

Find a Virtual Mentor: Reach out to mentors outside the company or within it via email, LinkedIn or other social platforms. Mentors can provide an invaluable resource for coaching and supporting you as a leader - not just providing feedback, but also sharing their own experiences and lessons learned.

Staying Current with Industry Trends & Best Practices

As a Sales Team Lead in a remote sales call center, it's crucial to stay informed about industry trends and best practices. Here are five ways you can do just that:

Attend virtual conferences - There are many virtual conferences related to the sales industry that take place throughout the year. Attending one or more of these events can help you stay up to date on the latest industry trends, as well as provide you with opportunities to network with other professionals.

Join online communities - There are plenty of online groups and forums dedicated to sales professionals. These can be great resources for staying current with the latest industry news and insights. Plus, engaging with other members can help you develop your own knowledge and share what you learn with your team.

Follow industry influencers and thought leaders - Keep tabs on social media accounts and blogs of thought leaders within your industry. Following these individuals can provide insight into emerging trends as well as best practices in sales.

Subscribe to publications and newsletters - There are several publications and newsletters dedicated to sales professionals, providing valuable content on industry trends, tips and techniques. Subscribing to these can keep you updated on the latest developments.

Hiring specialized consultants - Look for consulting agencies/experts who specialize in sales industry practices. They can analyze performances of teams, give feedback, suggest methodologies etc.

By continuously keeping yourself informed and up to date by utilizing these resources, you will be able to lead your sales team effectively towards maintaining optimal performance standards while doing so from any location around the world!